Contents

INTRODUCTION

Hunting is the perfect way to source healthy, high-quality meat. The Wild Game Cookbook will show you how to transform your harvest into flavorful feasts that your whole family will love.

From spicy Butter Duck to savory Slow Cooker Wild Boar Rag, this comprehensive wild game cookbook will give you everything you need to start simmering up something good, whether it be big game or small, waterfowl, upland birds, or game fish. There's even a helpful chapter on marinades, brines, rubs, sauces, and stocks to add mouthwatering flavor to your favorite proteins.

It has taken more than a decade to build, but there are almost 1000 recipes for wild game meat in this collection so far, and I am not even close to being done.

You will find recipes for pretty much every animal in North America that has a season and a bag limit, as well as some that don't, like jackrabbits.

A few pointers first. Wild game meat, strictly speaking, means meat that is hunted or trapped, ideally by a licensed hunter following all the legal rules. But other meats are considered "game meats," which is slightly different. For example, a deer someone hunted is wild game. Venison you bought at Whole Foods or wherever is not; it is, however a game meat. All wild game is "game meat," but not all game meats are wild game. Got it?

When it comes to venison, I am referring to all similar meats, so not only any deer, but also elk, moose, antelope, wild sheep, mountain goats, etc. All are very similar in the kitchen.

Game Tips

■ The meat of most game birds and animalsis significantly lower in saturated fat than that of their domestic counterparts. Quail, pheasant, and guinea hen all have 40 percent fewer calories and 60 percent less fat than chicken.

■ When you are cooking wild fowl, if the bird isn't young, use a moist-heat method for cooking it. Even if the bird is young, it is a good idea to serve the more-tender breast meat and save the rest for the stock pot to make gravy.

■ Most peopleovercook their game because they forget that there is less fat.

Native Game in North America

Big Game Small Game Game Birds

■Antelope■alligator ■ grouse

■ bear ■armadillo■ guineafowl

■Buffalo■ beaver ■partridge

■Caribou■ muskrat ■pheasant

■Deer■opossum ■ quail

■Elk■ porcupine ■squab (young pigeon)

■Moose■ rabbit ■ wild ducks

■Reindeer■ raccoon ■ wild geese

■Wild boar ■squirrel ■ wild turkey

WILD GAME RECIPES

Fillet of Buffalo with Applewood Bacon, Herb-Roasted Fingerling Potatoes, Caramelized Pearl Onions, and Gorgonzola-Sage Cream

Serves 6

Ingredients

- (6- to 8-ounce/170 to 225 g) buffalo fillets

- Salt and pepper

- 4 slices applewood-smoked bacon

- ½ pound (225 g) pearl onions, peeled

- 2 tablespoons (28 g) butter

- 1 teaspoon (4 g) sugar

Herb-Roasted Fingerling Potatoes

• 2 pounds (900 g) fingerling potatoes

• 2 tablespoons (30 ml) canola oil

• 2 tablespoons (5 g) chopped assorted

• fresh herbs

• Salt and pepper

Gorgonzola-Sage Cream

• 2 shallots, minced

• 1 teaspoon (5 g) butter

• 2 tablespoons (5 g) chopped fresh sage

• ½ cup (120 ml) white wine

• 2 cups (470 ml) heavy cream

• 2 ounces (57 g) gorgonzola cheese,

• Crumbled

• Juice of ½ lemon

• Salt and pepper

Directions

Heat a large (12-inch/30 cm) frying pan over high heat. Season the buffalo fillets with salt and pepper. Add the buffalo fillets to the hot pan and sear all sides until well browned. Wrap bacon around buffalo fillets and return to hot pan. Sear bacon on all sides until bacon is cooked and crisp and the buffalo is cooked to desired doneness. Cover loosely with foil and keep warm until ready to serve. In a frying pan, sauté onions in butter and sugar until golden brown.

Preheat oven to 350°F (180°C). Toss potatoes with oil and herbs. Season with salt and pepper. Roast on baking sheet for 20 to 30 minutes or until brown. Keep warm until ready to serve.

In a covered pan set over low heat, cook shallots in butter until softened but not browned. Add sage and wine. Bring to a boil and reduce by three-fourths. Add cream and reduce by half. Strain through a wire mesh strainer and discard solids. Add gorgonzola and lemon juice and whisk vigorously until smooth, or use an electric blender. Season with salt and pepper.

To serve, place beef, onions, and potatoes on a large platter or individual plates. Spoon the gorgonzola-sage sauce around beef

Duck Prosciutto with Caramelized Pears

Serves 6 to 8 as an appetizer

Ingredients

Duck prosciutto

- 2 tablespoons (12 g) whole allspice

- 1 tablespoon (6.6 g) dill seed

- 2 tablespoons (12 g) black peppercorns

- 1 stick cinnamon

- 1 tablespoon (5 g) whole coriander seeds

- ½ cup (73 g) brown sugar

- ½ cup (146 g) kosher salt

- 2 whole duck breasts, cut in half

Balsamic Glaze

• 1 cup (235 ml) balsamic vinegar

Caramelized Pears

• 2 large ripe pears (Bartlett or Bosc pears

• from Washington State are excellent)

• ½ lemon

• 3 tablespoons (42 g) unsalted butter

• ½ teaspoon (2 g) sugar

• Pinch of ground black pepper

Directions

Bring 4 cups (1 liter) of water to a boil. Add all ingredients to water except duck. Turn off heat and allow mixture to cool completely. Submerge duck in water/spice mixture and refrigerate 6 to 8 hours. Remove duck breasts from mixture and pat dry.

Light smoker with cedar chips and bring to 110°F (43°C). Smoke duck breast for 30 minutes. Remove from smoker and cool.

In a small saucepan set over medium-high heat, boil balsamic vinegar until reduced by one-half or until syrupy. Cool and refrigerate until ready to serve.

Peel and core the pears, then cut each one into four wedges. Rub them with lemon juice to keep them from discoloring. Melt butter in a medium (10-inch/25 cm) frying pan set over medium-high heat. Arrange the pears in the pan in a single layer and sprinkle with sugar. Cook 1½ minutes per side. Transfer to plate to cool.

To serve, fan the pears out on a warmed plate. Sprinkle lightly with ground black pepper. Cut very thin slices of Duck Prosciutto and place on plate alongside pear wedges. Drizzle with Balsamic Glaze and serve.

Grilled Venison Chop and Rabbit Sausage with Red Cabbage, Balsamic Vinegar, and Apples

Serves 2

Ingredients

Red Cabbage, Balsamic Vinegar, and Apples

• 1 tablespoon (15 ml) olive oil

• 1 onion, peeled and finely chopped

• 6 cups (420 g) thinly sliced red cabbage

• 2 apples, unpeeled, cored and diced into bite-sized pieces

• ½ cup (120 ml) water

• 2 tablespoons (30 ml) balsamic vinegar

• 2 tablespoons (30 ml) red wine vinegar

• 1 teaspoon (6 g) coarse salt

Venison Chop and Rabbit Sausage

• ¼ cup (60 ml) extra-virgin olive oil

• 2 garlic cloves, minced

• 1 heaping teaspoon (1 g) chopped fresh rosemary

• 1 (8-ounce/225 g) venison chop

• 1 tablespoon (5 g) dried green peppercorns

• 6 ounces (170 g) rabbit sausage

Directions

Heat oil in large skillet over medium heat and add onion and cabbage. Sauté until onion is soft, about 5 minutes. Add apples, water, vinegars, and salt. Cook for an additional 20 minutes, or until cabbage is just barely tender. Cover and keep hot until ready to serve.

Place olive oil, garlic, and rosemary in a bowl. Add venison chop and marinate for 30 minutes. Heat grill to high. Remove venison chop from marinade and coat with peppercorns. Grill venison chop for 8 to 10 minutes or until chop is browned on the outside and juicy pink on the inside. Cook sausage until the outside is brown and the juices run clear.

To serve, place some red cabbage mixture on each plate. Cut the grilled venison chop meat away from the bone. Carve meat on the bias into thin slices. Slice rabbit sausage into bitesize pieces. Top each plate with half the grilled venison chop slices and half the rabbit sausage pieces.

Pan-Seared Hudson Valley Foie Gras, Toasted Brioche, Pear-Shallot Compote, and Port Wine–Fig Syrup

Serves 2

Ingredients

- Pear-Shallot Compote

- 1 tablespoon (14 g) butter

- 2 ripe pears, peeled, cored and diced

- 1 shallot, peeled and minced

- 1 teaspoon (2 g) minced fresh ginger

- 2 ounces (60 ml) white wine

- 2 ounces (60 ml) champagne vinegar

- 2 ounces (60 ml) honey

- Salt and pepper

Port Wine–Fig syrup

- 1 cup (235 ml) port wine

- 2 dried black figs, minced

Foie Gras

- 1 teaspoon (5 g) butter

- 2 (2-ounce/55 g) portions Hudson Valley foie gras (duck liver)

- 2 (3-inch/7.5 cm) triangles brioche or light yeast bread, crust removed, toasted

Directions

Heat a medium (10-inch/25 cm) frying pan set over medium heat. Melt butter and sauté pears, shallot, and ginger until pears are very soft. Add wine, vinegar, and honey. Simmer gently for 10 minutes on medium heat. Season with salt and pepper.

Combine port wine and figs in a small saucepan and simmer until syrupy. Strain through a fine mesh strainer, discarding the solids.

Heat a small (6-inch/15 cm) frying pan set over medium-high heat. Melt butter in the hot pan. While butter is still sizzling, add the foie gras and sear on both sides until light golden brown. The foie gras should be rare.

To serve, spoon some pear-shallot compote in center of each plate. Place brioche on top of compote. Place foie gras on top of brioche. Drizzle port wine–fig syrup around the foie gras.

Five-Spice Peking Duck Breast with Nori with Sticky Rice, and Cilantro Ponzu Sauce

Serves 2

Ingredients

Peking Duck

- 2 duck breasts, skin on

- Cinnamon, to season

- Clove, to season

- Fennel seed, to season

- Star anise, to season

- Black pepper, to season

Nori with Sticky Rice

- 2 sheets seaweed wrapper (nori)

- Sushi rice, seasoned and prepared according to package instructions

- 1 small cucumber, peeled, seeded, and sliced into matchsticks

- 1 small red bell pepper, cored and sliced into matchsticks

- 1 small yellow bell pepper, cored and sliced into matchsticks

Cilantro Ponzu Sauce

- ¼ cup (60 ml) soy sauce

- 2 tablespoons (30 ml) water

- 1 tablespoon (15 ml) rice wine vinegar

- 1 ounce (28 ml) fresh orange juice

- 2 teaspoons (4 g) freshly grated ginger

- ½ jalapeño, stem and ribs removed, minced

- 1 tablespoon (1 g) minced fresh cilantro

Directions

Score the skin side of duck breast with a very sharp knife so it will render some fat and the skin will get crispy. Season both sides of duck with five spices.

Heat a cast-iron or other heavy frying pan over medium-high heat. Place the duck breasts into the hot pan skin-side down and cook until skin turns very deep golden brown and some fat has accumulated in the pan. Flip the duck breast over in the pan and cook until medium-rare (the meat is not yet fi rm but springs back quickly when pressed with a finger) or medium (the meat is somewhat fi rm to the touch). Keep warm until ready to serve.

Toast and soften the nori sheets by holding briefly over a lit burner on stovetop. Spread sushi rice over the width and one half the length of each nori sheet. Place some cucumber, red bell pepper, and yellow bell pepper slices across the width of the rice. Roll the nori up and over the rice and vegetables, tucking the ends in, to make a tight cylinder. Slice nori rolls on an angle before serving.

In small bowl, combine all sauce ingredients and mix well.

To serve, carve the duck breast into ¼-inch (1 cm) slices, fan them across a platter or serving plates, add the sliced nori rolls, and drizzle the ponzu sauce over the duck and nori rolls and around the plate.

Porcini-Crusted Venison, Yukon Gold Potato and Celery Root Gratin, Wild Mushroom Ragout, and Sauce Perigueux

Serves 2

Ingredients

Porcini-crusted venison

- ¼ cup (56 g) porcini mushroom powder

- (6- to 8-ounce/170 to 225 g) venison sirloin steaks

- Salt and pepper

Yukon Gold Potato and Celery Root Gratin

• 1-pound (450 g) Yukon gold potatoes, sliced thin

• 1-pound (450 g) celery root, sliced thin

• 1 teaspoon (3 g) minced garlic

• 1 cup (235 ml) heavy cream

• ¼ cup (20 g) grated asiago cheese

• Salt and pepper to taste

Wild Mushroom Ragout

• 2 tablespoons (30 ml) olive oil

• 3 tablespoons (30 g) minced shallots

• 1-pound (450 g) portobello mushrooms, sliced

• ¼ cup (45 g) finely diced tomatoes

• ¼ cup (60 ml) vegetable or chicken broth

• ¼ cup (60 ml) heavy cream

• 2 tablespoons (5 g) chopped fresh herbs

Sauce Perigueux

• 1 shallot, chopped

• 1 sprig thyme

- 1 tablespoon (14 g) butter

- ½ cup (120 ml) red wine

- 3 cups (700 ml) veal or beef stock, reduced to ½ cup (120 ml)

- Truffle slices (omit if not available)

Directions

Preheat grill to high. Sprinkle porcini mushroom powder on venison, season with salt and pepper, and grill to desired doneness. Cover loosely with foil and keep warm until ready to serve.

Preheat oven to 350°F (180°C). Layer sliced potatoes and celery root in a 9 x 13-inch (23 x 33 cm) baking dish. Add garlic and cream, sprinkle with Asiago cheese, and season with salt and pepper. Bake for 45 minutes or until bubbling and potatoes and celery root are tender when pierced with a knife. Cover with parchment paper. Place another pan of approximately the same size over the top and weigh it down with a couple of cans from the pantry. Allow to cool. Cut into square or triangular shapes when ready to serve.

Heat olive oil and shallots in a frying pan set on medium-high heat. Add sliced mushrooms and toss in the pan. Cook mushrooms until soft and fragrant, about 4 minutes. Add tomatoes, broth, heavy cream, and chopped herbs. Cook on medium-high until reduced enough that the sauce coats the back of a spoon. Keep warm.

In a covered sauté pan over low heat, cook shallot and thyme in butter until softened but not browned. Add red wine and reduce by three-fourths. Add stock and reduce. Add sliced black truffles.

To serve, put a slice of potato gratin in the center of each plate and spoon some mushroom ragout on top of gratin. Place steak next to potato gratin on each plate and spoon sauce around the steak.

Prosciutto-Wrapped Pheasant Breast with Root Vegetable Hash, Frisée, and Granny Smith Apple Gastrique

Serves 4

Ingredients

Prosciutto-Wrapped Pheasant Breasts

- 4 whole skinless, boneless pheasant breasts
- Salt and pepper
- 4 thin slices prosciutto

Root Vegetable Hash

- 1 tablespoon (14 g) butter
- 2 medium sweet potatoes, peeled and diced
- 2 medium Yukon gold potatoes, peeled and diced
- 4 medium carrots, peeled and diced

• 2 medium turnips or rutabagas, peeled and diced

• 1 shallot, peeled and minced

• 1 clove garlic, peeled and minced

• 1 tablespoon (2.5 g) chopped fresh herbs

Granny Smith Apple Gastrique

• 1 cup (226 g) sugar

• ⅔ cup (160 ml) cider vinegar

• 1 cup (235 ml) fresh green apple juice

• 3 sprigs fresh thyme

• 4 cups (1 liter) chicken stock

Frisée

• ¼ pound (115 g) frisée greens, washed and dried

• Champagne vinegar, to taste

• Salt and pepper

Directions

Heat grill to medium. Season pheasant breasts with small amount of salt and pepper. Wrap breasts in prosciutto. Grill on both sides until prosciutto is well-seared and the pheasant is cooked medium-rare (the breast meat will spring back quickly when pressed with a finger). Cover loosely with aluminum foil and keep warm until ready to serve.

Heat butter in a large (12-inch/30 cm) frying pan set over medium heat. Sauté vegetables until soft but not mushy. Add shallot, garlic, and herbs, sauté for 3 minutes longer, stirring gently, and cool.

Melt sugar in a heavy-bottomed pan until it turns golden brown. Add vinegar, apple juice, thyme, and stock. Simmer until mixture thickens slightly.

Season the frisée with a small amount of champagne vinegar, season lightly with salt and pepper.

To serve, divide the root vegetable hash among four plates. Place some dressed frisée on top of hash. Place pheasant breast on each plate and drizzle with gastrique.

Grilled Elk Chop, Roasted Garlic Custard, Oregon Hazelnuts, Winter Squash Ratatouille, and Pan Sauce

Serves 2

Ingredients

Elk Chops

- 1 tablespoon (4.3 g) dried juniper berries

- 1 tablespoon (1.3 g) mixed dried herbs

- (like herbs de Provence or fines herbs)

- ¼ cup (60 ml) olive oil

- 2 large elk chops

- 3 cups (705 ml) lamb or beef stock

- ½ sprig fresh rosemary

Roasted Garlic Custard

- 2 to 3 cloves garlic

- Butter to grease ramekins

- 1 cup (235 ml) heavy cream

- 1 egg

- 1 egg yolk

- Salt and pepper

Winter Squash Ratatouille

- 1 tablespoon (15 ml) olive oil

- ¼ cup (35 g) finely diced acorn squash

- ¼ cup (35 g) finely diced butternut squash

- ¼ cup (20.5 g) finely diced eggplant, peeled

- ¼ cup (37 g) finely diced red bell pepper

- 1 clove garlic, minced

- 1 shallot, minced

- ½ cup (90 g) seeded and finely chopped plum tomato

- Mixed herbs of your choice

- Salt and pepper

- Hazelnuts, chopped and toasted

Directions

In a bowl or deep-sided pan combine juniper berries, mixed herbs, and olive oil. Combine well. Add elk chops to the pan and turn to coat completely. Refrigerate, covered, for several hours or overnight. Turn the chops over in the herbed oil every few hours.

Meanwhile, in a small saucepan set on medium, slowly reduce the stock to about ¼ cup (60 ml) or until slightly syrupy. Add the rosemary about 30 minutes before the reduction is done. Keep covered and warm.

Remove elk chops from refrigerator 1 hour before cooking so they warm up to room temperature. Preheat grill to medium-high. Scrape excess oil from elk chops and grill to desired doneness (medium-rare recommended). Keep warm until ready to serve.

Preheat oven to 300°F (150°C). Wrap garlic loosely in a small foil pouch and bake for 40 to 50 minutes, or until garlic is soft. Remove skin and mash with a fork.

Coat two 6-ounce (175 ml) ramekins with butter. Combine roasted garlic purée and remaining ingredients. Pour into buttered ramekins. (There will be a little mixture left over.) Cook in a water bath in oven. Check after 30 minutes. Remove from oven when the centers of the mixture wiggle only slightly when you shake the pan.

Heat oil in a large frying pan over medium-high heat. Sauté the squash, eggplant, red bell pepper, garlic, and shallots for 4 to 5 minutes. Add the tomato and herbs and simmer uncovered until the squash is tender. Season with salt and pepper.

To serve, place some ratatouille on each dinner plate. Place elk chop on top. Run a knife around the inside of the ramekins to loosen the custard; invert onto plate. Sprinkle with hazelnuts and drizzle with pan sauce.

Quail with Braised Greens and Lemon-Thyme Vinaigrette

Serves 4

Ingredients

Quail

- 4 boneless quail

- Salt and pepper

- 1 tablespoon (15 ml) vegetable oil

Braised Greens

- 1 tablespoon (15 ml) olive oil

- 4 cups (268 g) roughly chopped kale, red chard, mustard greens, and chicory greens

- 1 tablespoon (10 g) minced shallot

- 1 teaspoon (3 g) minced garlic

- ½ cup (120 ml) chicken stock

- Salt and pepper

- 1 tablespoon (14 g) butter

Lemon-Thyme Vinaigrette

- 2 tablespoons (20 g) minced shallot

- 1 teaspoon (3 g) minced garlic

- 2 tablespoons (5 g) chopped fresh thyme

- 2 ounces (56 ml) fresh lemon juice

- 1 teaspoon (5 g) Dijon mustard

- 2 ounces (56 ml) champagne vinegar

- 6 ounces (168 ml) olive oil

- Salt and pepper

Directions

Preheat oven to 400°F (200°C). Season quail with salt and pepper. Heat vegetable oil in a large (12-inch/30 cm) frying pan until barely smoking. Add quail to hot oil and sear until skin is crispy. Transfer to baking sheet and roast in oven until cooked through, about 20 to 25 minutes. Cover loosely with foil and keep warm until ready to serve.

Heat olive oil in a large pot. Add greens and sauté until wilted. Add shallots and garlic and cook for another minute while tossing. Add chicken stock and cook until greens are tender, about 20 minutes. Season with salt and pepper. Add butter and toss.

Combine all vinaigrette ingredients except oil, salt, and pepper. Slowly add oil while whisking vigorously. The mixture will thicken as you go along. Season with salt and pepper.

To serve, spoon braised greens onto a platter, slice quail about ½-inch (1.25 cm) thick and place on top, and spoon some vinaigrette over quail. Serve with mixed grain pilaf or couscous.

Mocha Espresso Flan with Caramel Sauce and English Toffee

Serves 6

Ingredients

Caramel Sauce

- 3 cups (600 g) granulated sugar

- 1 cup (235 ml) water

- Dash lemon juice

- 2 cups (470 ml) whipping cream

English Toffee

- 2 cups (400 g) sugar

- ½ pound (225 g) butter

- ¼ cup (60 ml) water

- Vanilla to taste

Flan

- 3½ cups (822 ml) heavy cream

- 6 ounces (170 g) granulated sugar

- 4 egg yolks

- 3 eggs

- 1 teaspoon (5g) mocha paste*

- ¼ cup (60 ml) espresso

* Mocha paste can be found in professional-baking-supply houses. In a pinch, substitute 1 teaspoon (3 g) cocoa.

Directions

Combine all Caramel Sauce ingredients except cream in a saucepan and bring to a boil. Continue cooking until the temperature registers 320°F (160°C) on a candy thermometer. Slowly whisk in cream and lower heat. Keep warm until ready to serve.

Combine all toffee ingredients in a saucepan and cook until mixture registers 300°F (150°C) on a candy thermometer. Pour onto rimmed metal baking sheet, cool completely, and chop into small pieces to use as garnish.

For flan, preheat oven to 350°F (180°C). Combine cream and sugar in a saucepan and bring to a boil. Remove from heat and gradually add the egg yolks and eggs while whisking constantly. Mix in mocha paste and espresso.

Spoon mixture into ramekins and place in roasting pan large enough to fit all ramekins without touching. Fill pan with hot tap water so that water comes halfway up the sides of ramekins. Bake until custard is set (approximately 25 minutes). Test by inserting a knife into the center of one flan; it should come out just slightly wet. Cool on countertop, then refrigerate at least 3 hours.

To serve, run a small knife around the edge of each flan to loosen from the ramekins. Invert ramekins onto individual dessert plates and slowly lift away to un-mold flans. Pour caramel sauce over flans and sprinkle with crushed English toffee.

Venison Tenderloin with Sherried Mushrooms

Serves 4 to 6

Ingredients

Venison

- 3 tablespoons (45 ml) olive oil

- 3 tablespoons (45 ml) liquid smoke

- 1 tablespoon (18 g) kosher salt

- 1 tablespoon (7 g) freshly ground black pepper

- 2 venison tenderloins

Sherried mushrooms

- ½ pound (225 g) crimini mushrooms, cleaned and sliced

- 4 tablespoons (56 g) butter

- Seasoning salt (Alpine Touch or Johnny's Seasoning Salt are recommended, or combine salt, garlic powder, pepper, and paprika)

- 2 tablespoons (30 ml) sherry cooking wine

- 3 cups (700 ml) heavy cream

- 1 pound (450 g) uncooked fettuccine, cooked according to package directions

Directions

In a large bowl, combine olive oil, liquid smoke, salt, and pepper. Marinate tenderloins in mixture for approximately 30 minutes.

Preheat grill to high. Wipe excess marinade from the tenderloins and grill until medium-rare to medium.

In a medium frying pan, sauté mushrooms in butter until well-browned but not dry. Add seasoning salt, sherry, and heavy cream. Mix ingredients and reduce until thick enough to coat the back of a spoon.

Slice venison tenderloins about ½-inch (1.25 cm) thick and place on a bed of fettuccine. Spoon the sherried mushrooms and cream sauce over the tenderloins and fettuccini.

Wine pairing: Lindemans Bin 40 Merlot 2004

Elk Empanada

Makes about 16 two-bite pastries

Ingredients

- 2 tablespoons (30 ml) vegetable oil

- 1½ pounds (680 g) ground elk

- ½ cup (80 g) finely chopped onion

- 1 tablespoon (8.5 g) minced garlic

- 1 tablespoon (18 g) salt

- ½ tablespoon (3.2 g) pepper

- ½ tablespoon (1 g) sage

- 2 tablespoons (30 ml) Worcestershire sauce

- 1 yam, finely chopped (1½ cups/225 g)

- 1 apple, finely chopped (1½ cups/165 g)

- ¼ cup (32 g) cornstarch

- 1 cup (235 ml) apple cider

- 12 ounces (355 ml) beer

- 1 package frozen puff pastry dough

- 1 egg, beaten

Directions

Preheat oven to 400°F (200°C). In a large frying pan set over high heat, heat oil and sauté elk, onion, garlic, salt, pepper, sage, and Worcestershire sauce until elk is cooked and onion is tender. Add yam, apple, cornstarch, apple cider, and beer. Simmer approximately 10 minutes, or until yams are tender. Transfer to a bowl and let cool.

Follow manufacturer's instructions for thawing puff pastry. Cut each puff pastry sheet into 8 squares. Brush the outside edges of the puff pastry squares with beaten egg. Place a heaping tablespoon of elk filling in center of each square and fold over diagonally. Crimp edges with fork to seal. Brush remaining egg on top of pastries. Bake 10 minutes, or until pastry is golden brown.

Serve as hors d'oeuvres, or as a light luncheon with a tossed green salad.

Wild Turkey and Wild Rice Soup

Serves six

Ingredients

- 2 tablespoons (30 ml) vegetable oil

- 1 cup (100 g) green onion, finely chopped

- 1½ cups (180 g) celery, diced

- ½ cup (74.5 g) red bell pepper, diced

- ¼ cup (27.5 g) grated carrot

- 1 to 1½ pounds (450 to 680 g) wild turkey breast meat, cut into ½-inch (1.25 cm) dice

- 4 cups (1 liter) water

- 2 tablespoons (30 ml) chicken bouillon

- 1 8-ounce (225 g) box long grain and wild rice mix, with seasoning

- 1 large fi rm apple (Granny Smith works well), peeled and cut into ½-inch (1.25 cm) dice

Directions

In a 4-quart or other large saucepan, heat the vegetable oil and sauté green onion, celery, red bell pepper, and carrots until tender, about 3 minutes. Add wild turkey breast, water, and chicken bouillon. Simmer 15 minutes or until turkey is cooked.

Meanwhile, cook 1 box long grain and wild rice with seasoning. Add cooked rice and apple to soup and simmer for just 5 minutes, until apple is warm but still crisp. Serve immediately.

Variation: Substitute apple with 1½ cups (234 g) sautéed mushrooms and 1 cup (235 ml) heavy cream.

Grilled Mallard with Plum Sauce

Serves four

Ingredients

Plum Sauce

- 1 (8-ounce/225 g) jar plum jelly

- 2 tablespoons (31 g) yellow mustard

• 2 tablespoons (30 g) horseradish

• Juice of 1 lemon

Grilled Mallard

• 1½ to 2 pounds (680 to 907 g) mallard duck breast meat, skin removed

• 2 tablespoons (17 g) minced garlic

• 1 tablespoon (18 g) Greek-style seasoning

• 1 cup (235 ml) Worcestershire sauce

• 1 (16-ounce/475 ml) bottle Italian salad dressing

• ½ bottle sweet and sour hot sauce (optional)

• Bacon slices, as needed

• Seasoned pepper blend (available in supermarkets)

• 1 cup (230 g) hickory wood grilling chips, soaked in water at least 1 hour

Directions

Combine sauce ingredients and stir over medium heat until jelly melts. Reserve until ready to serve. Reheat gently before serving.

Rub duck breasts with minced garlic, then sprinkle liberally with Greek seasoning. Combine Worcestershire sauce, Italian dressing, and sweet and sour hot sauce (if using) and pour over duck breasts. Marinate at least 3 hours.

Light charcoal grill with a generous amount of fuel. Wait for the fi re to develop an even white ash overall. Just before cooking, tightly wrap 1 slice of bacon around each breast and sprinkle with seasoned pepper. Add a small handful of hickory chips to the fire. Grill with heavy smoke until bacon is golden brown. Breasts are best served medium-rare. Do not overcook. Add more chips if needed. Drizzle plum sauce over grilled breast and serve hot.

Wild rice, asparagus, and spiced apples are recommended side dishes.

Grilled Mallard Hors d'oeuvres

Yields about 28 hors d'oeuvres

Ingredients

Plum Sauce

- 1 (8-ounce/225 g) jar plum jelly

- 2 tablespoons (31 g) yellow mustard

- 2 tablespoons (30 g) horseradish

- Juice of 1 lemon

Grilled Mallard

- 1½ to 2 pounds (680 to 907 g) mallard duck breast meat, skin removed

- 2 tablespoons (17 g) minced garlic

- 1 tablespoon (18 g) Greek-style seasoning

- 1 cup (235 ml) Worcestershire sauce

- 1 (16-ounce/475 ml) bottle Italian salad dressing

- ½ bottle sweet and sour hot sauce (optional)

- Bacon slices, as needed

- Seasoned pepper blend (available in supermarkets)

- 1 cup (230 g) hickory wood grilling chips, soaked in water at least 1 hour

Venison Backstraps with Garlic Sautéed Mushrooms

Serves 6 to 10

Ingredients

Backstraps

- Backstraps from 1 deer (1 whole beef tenderloin may be substituted)

- 8 to 10 cloves garlic, peeled and minced

- Greek-style seasoning

- 1 (15-ounce/440 ml) bottle Worcestershire sauce

- 1 cup (235 ml) extra-virgin olive oil

- 2 (5-ounce/150 ml) bottles hot red pepper sauce

• 1 bottle sweet and sour hot sauce

Garlic Sautéed Mushrooms

• 2 heaping tablespoons (17 g) minced garlic

• ½ pound (225 g) butter

• ½ cup (120 ml) soy sauce

• 1 pound (450 g) fresh mushrooms, sliced

Directions

Thoroughly clean and trim backstraps. Be sure all ligaments and silver skin are removed. Rub liberally with garlic, then sprinkle liberally with Greek-style seasoning and pat into meat. Cut backstraps in half and place in a large container. Sprinkle liberally with Worcestershire sauce, then gently "flood" with olive oil (the olive oil will wash off the Greek seasoning and garlic if you're not careful; you can hold a spoon directly over the meat and flood across the spoon).

Next, pour 2 bottles of hot red pepper sauce and 1 bottle of sweet and sour hot sauce over top of backstraps. Let marinate 1 to 2 hours, then mix meat with marinade to cover thoroughly, and let sit another 30 minutes to 1 hour.

Light charcoal grill with a generous amount of fuel. When the fi re is ready, grill the backstraps to your satisfaction (medium-rare to medium recommended).

In a frying pan set over medium heat, combine garlic, butter, and soy sauce. Heat until mixture simmers, then add mushrooms. Sauté to desired texture.

Wild rice, asparagus, and either candied carrots or a pineapple casserole are nice side dishes.

Goose Pie

Serves 2 to 4 hungry hunters, or a family of 4 to 6

Ingredients

• 2 geese, quartered into legs and breasts

• ½ cup (80 g) chopped onions

• 4 beef bouillon cubes

- 1 garlic clove, minced

- 1 teaspoon (5 ml) Worcestershire sauce

- 2 tablespoons (3 g) Dymond Lake Seasoning (see recipe below)

- 2 cups (300 g) peeled and diced potatoes

- 1 cup (128 g) diced carrots

- ¼ cup (31 g) flour

- 1 cup (235 ml) cold water

- 1 (10-inch/26 cm) pie shell, top and bottom crusts, uncooked

Dymond Lake Seasoning

- 1 teaspoon (1.7 g) seasoned pepper (available in supermarkets)

- 1 teaspoon (2 g) celery salt

- 1 tablespoon (3.8 g) parsley

- ½ teaspoon (0.9 g) oregano

- ½ teaspoon (0.7 g) basil

- ½ teaspoon (0.5 g) thyme

- Salt to taste

Directions

Place geese, onions, beef bouillon cubes, garlic, Worcestershire sauce, and Dymond Lake Seasoning in a large Dutch oven and cover with water. Simmer until meat falls off leg bones, about 3 to 4 hours. Let cool, then remove meat from bones. Discard any meat that is still tough. Chop up breasts if they have not already fallen apart. Return meat to broth in Dutch oven and add potatoes and carrots. Cook until vegetables are tender, about 30 minutes.

Preheat oven to 425°F (220°C). Taste to check the seasoning and add a little salt or more Dymond Lake Seasoning if desired. Blend flour into cold water by shaking it in a jar or using a hand blender. Stir into mixture in Dutch oven and simmer while stirring for about 2 minutes. Pour mixture into pie shell. Cover with top crust, cut slits to allow the steam to escape, and bake for 10 minutes. Lower heat to 375°F (190°C) and bake for an additional 40 minutes.

Variation: Add ½ cup (65 g) diced turnips and 1 (10-ounce/ 280 g) can of mushrooms.

Serve with cranberry sauce or a nice chili sauce, tossed salad, and crusty rolls.

This pie freezes very well, baked or unbaked. If unbaked, thaw it before baking and increase the final baking time if necessary—it's best bubbling hot in the middle with a nicely browned crust. If baked before freezing, just heat through until hot and bubbly.

Spicy Game Chili

Serves 10 to 12

Ingredients

- 3 pounds (1.4 kg) game meat (moose, caribou, venison, elk, or a combination)

- 3 tablespoons (45 ml) vegetable oil, divided

- 1 cup (235 ml) water

- 2 medium onions, peeled and sliced thin

- 2 green peppers, ribs and seeds removed, cut into strips

- 2 red bell peppers, ribs and seeds removed, cut into strips

- 2 jalapeño chilies, ribs and seeds removed, finely chopped (optional)

- 4 garlic cloves, chopped or crushed

- 2 teaspoons (4.2 g) ground cumin

- 1 teaspoon (1.8 g) cayenne pepper (or more to taste)

- 2 teaspoons (12.6 g) salt

- 2 cups (475 ml) beef stock

- 2 (14.5-ounce/410 g) cans crushed or puréed tomatoes

- 2 (15-ounce/425 g) cans kidney beans

Directions

Cut meat into strips. In a large skillet, heat 2 tablespoons (30 ml) of oil over medium-high heat. Add meat and sauté until strips begin to brown. Add water to pan. Set aside. In a large pot, heat 1 tablespoon (15 ml) of oil. Add onions and cook for 3 minutes. Add peppers, jalapeños, and garlic. Cook another 5 minutes or until softened. Add spices, salt, beef stock, cooked meat, and tomatoes. Bring to a boil. Turn down heat to medium-low and simmer for 1 hour or until meat is tender. Add kidney beans. Simmer for 15 minutes longer.

For thinner chili, add more stock and crushed tomatoes.

Handling Your Game

■ An animal should beeviscerated within an hour of harvest and meat refrigerated within a few hours. Meat will damageor be ruined if it's not dressed, transported, and chilled properly

Baked Stuffed Caribou Heart

Serves 2

Ingredients

- 1 caribou heart

- 1 quart (1 liter) cold water

- ¼ cup (73 g) kosher salt

- 1 cup (108 g) dry bread crumbs

- 1 onion, chopped

- ½ teaspoon (3 g) salt

- ½ teaspoon (0.75 g) savory or poultry seasoning

- 4 teaspoons (20 ml) melted butter

- Salt pork

Directions

Wipe heart clean. Combine water and salt in a large pan and soak heart overnight.

Preheat oven to 325°F (170°C). Trim blood vessels and fat from heart. Combine bread crumbs, onion, salt, seasoning, and melted butter to make dressing. Stuff cavity with dressing; skewer or sew up heart. Place in roasting pan and lay strips of salt pork over heart. Add 1 cup (235 ml) water to pan. Cover and bake for 3 hours or until tender.

BBQ Caribou Ribs

Serves 4

Ingredients

- 3 tablespoons (45 ml) cooking oil

- 4 pounds (1.81 kg) caribou ribs, cut into 3- or 4-rib pieces

- 1 cup (235 ml) ketchup

- 1 cup (235 ml) water

- 2 tablespoons (30 ml) vinegar

- 1 tablespoon (15 ml) lemon juice

- 1 tablespoon (15 ml) Worcestershire sauce

- 1 tablespoon (15 ml) prepared mustard

- 3 tablespoons (45 g) brown sugar

- 1 teaspoon (6 g) salt

- ¼ teaspoon (0.5 g) pepper

Directions

Preheat oven to 350°F (180°C). In a large frying pan, heat oil until barely smoking. Add ribs and sauté until brown. Transfer ribs to a greased baking dish. Add remaining ingredients to pan and bring to boil for 1 minute. Pour mixture over ribs. Cover with foil and bake until tender, about 2 hours.

Where's It from and what's It Taste Like?

■ Caribou (reindeer) live primarily in North America and Siberia. Their meat is sweeter than that of other venison.

Bourbon Buffalo Pheasant Strips

Serves 2

Ingredients

• ½ yellow onion, diced

• 2 tablespoons (28 g) butter

• ¼ cup (60 ml) bourbon

• ⅓cup (75 g) brown sugar

• ⅔cup (160 ml) Frank's Red-Hot Sauce or other hot red pepper sauce

• 1 cup (125 g) flour

• 1 tablespoon (18 g) salt

• 1 teaspoon (2 g) black pepper

• 4 to 5 skinless pheasant breasts

• Oil for frying

• Ranch or blue cheese dressing for dipping

Directions

Place onion and butter in frying pan and cook over medium-high heat until onions become translucent (approximately 3 minutes). Remove pan from heat and add bourbon. Ignite with match or lighter and let flames subside.

Return pan to stove. Stir in brown sugar and cook on low heat until sugar has dissolved. Add hot red pepper sauce and simmer on low heat for a few minutes.

Combine flour, salt, and black pepper in a shallow bowl or pan. Check pheasant breasts for shot. Cut breasts into strips (approximately 5 per breast). Dredge the strips in seasoned flour.

Heat oil 2 inches (5 cm) deep in large heavy-bottomed pan to 360°F (185°C) or until a small piece of bread fries instantly when dropped into the oil. Shake excess flour off pheasant strips and fry in oil until golden brown. Toss strips with bourbon sauce and serve with ranch or blue cheese dressing for dipping.

Grilled Pheasant Breast over Parmesan Potato Risotto with Spiced Wine Demi-Glace

Serves 6

Ingredients

Spiced Wine Demi-Glace

- ½ bottle (375 ml) port wine

- ½ bottle (375 ml) red wine

- 2 (14-ounce/395 ml) cans beef broth

- 2 cinnamon sticks

- 2 ounces (55 g) orange juice concentrate, thawed

- 2 packets beef gravy mix

Potato Risotto

- 6 medium russet potatoes, peeled and diced into very small cubes

- Water for boiling, lightly salted

- 2 tablespoons (28 g) butter

- 1 pint (475 ml) heavy cream

- Salt and pepper

- 1 cup (80 g) shredded Parmesan cheese

- Fresh herbs (optional)

Pheasant Breast

- 12 boneless, skinless pheasant breasts

- 2 tablespoons (28 g) butter, softened

- Salt and pepper

Directions

Bring port wine and red wine to a boil and reduce by three-fourths. Add beef broth, cinnamon sticks, and orange juice. Bring to a boil. Add gravy mix slowly until sauce begins to thicken. (It may not be necessary to use all of mix.) Reduce heat and simmer 15 minutes or to desired thickness. Remove cinnamon sticks and keep sauce covered in a warm place until ready to use.

In a large pot, place potatoes in lightly salted water to cover and bring to a simmer. Cook potatoes until al dente, remove from heat, and drain. Run cold water over the potatoes to stop the cooking. Place butter in a large sauté pan on medium-high heat and add potatoes. Sauté potatoes a few minutes, stirring only once or twice, and then add heavy cream. Add salt and pepper to taste and reduce cream until it begins to thicken. Toss in Parmesan cheese and heat until thickened and well combined. Add fresh herbs like rosemary or thyme if desired. Remove from heat and serve immediately.

Preheat grill to medium. Brush pheasant breast with softened butter and season with salt and pepper. Place on hot grill. (You may sear in frying pan if grill is not available.) Grill pheasant until done, about 3 minutes per side, making sure not to overcook. Serve immediately over potato risotto and drizzle with spiced wine sauce. Serve with vegetable of your choice.

Maple-Glazed Bacon-Wrapped Chukar

Serves six

Ingredients

• 12 chukar breasts (pheasant may be substituted, but use 6 to 8 breasts)

• 12 to 14 strips thick-cut smoked bacon

- ½ cup (120 ml) pure maple syrup

Directions

Preheat oven to 400°F (200°C). Cut each chukar in half lengthwise, yielding 24 pieces. Cut the bacon strips in half and wrap each piece of chukar. It may be necessary to fold the chukar in half so that it fits into the bacon when wrapped up. Place wrapped chukar on greased or parchment paper–covered baking sheet. Bake in oven until bacon is nearly done (meat will feel fi rm but springy when pressed with a finger).

Remove from oven and brush each piece with maple syrup. Place back in oven and bake until finished, about 5 more minutes (remove before syrup begins to burn). Brush once more with syrup and let cool slightly. Serve on platter with frilly toothpicks.

Spicy Elk and Lentil Stew

Serves 6

Ingredients

• 8 slices thick-cut smoked bacon, diced

• 1 pound (0.5 kg) cubed elk, deer, or venison top round

• 1 medium onion, chopped

• 2 chipotle peppers in adobo sauce (available from gourmet supermarkets)

• 1 (14½-ounce /410 g can-diced tomatoes

• 1 celery rib, diced

• 1 carrot, diced

• 3 garlic cloves, minced

• Salt and pepper to taste

• 4 tablespoons (60 ml) olive oil

• 2 packed tablespoons (28 g) light brown sugar

• 2 tablespoons (15 g) chili powder

• 1 tablespoon (7 g) paprika

• 2 teaspoons (5 g) ground cumin

- ½ teaspoon (1 g) cayenne pepper, or to taste

- 2 teaspoons (2 g) dried oregano, crumbled

- 1 sprig fresh or ½ teaspoon (0.5 g) dried thyme

- 1 (6-ounce/170 g) can tomato paste

- 1 teaspoon (4 g) dry mustard

- 2 cups lentils (284 g), rinsed and drained

- 3 bay leaves

- 8 cups (2 liters) chicken stock or low sodium chicken broth

Directions

Cook bacon in 5- to 6-quart (5- to 6-liter) pot over medium-high heat until fat melts. Add cubed elk and cook for 5 minutes, stirring occasionally. Add onion, chipotle peppers, tomatoes, celery, carrots, garlic, salt, pepper, and oil, stirring occasionally, until vegetables soften (approximately 5 minutes).

Meanwhile, stir together brown sugar, chili powder, paprika, cumin, cayenne pepper, oregano, thyme, tomato paste, and mustard. Add mixture to pot and cook, stirring gently until fragrant (approximately 4 minutes). Add lentils, bay leaves, and stock. Simmer uncovered, stirring occasionally, until lentils are very soft (approximately 50 to 60 minutes). Discard bay leaves before serving.

Peppered Grilled Elk Medallions with Red Wine Sauce and Lingonberry Compote

Serves 6

Ingredients

Red Wine Sauce

- 1 (750 ml) bottle red wine

- 2 (14-ounce/425 ml) cans beef broth

- 1 to 2 packets beef gravy mix

- 1 fresh rosemary sprig

Lingonberry Compote

- 2 cups (500 g) frozen lingonberries (lingonberries may be available at

- gourmet supermarkets; another berry may be substituted)

- 1 (6-ounce/175 ml) can pineapple juice

- ½ to 1 cup (100 to 200 g) granulated sugar

- 3 tablespoons (24 g) cornstarch, mixed with an equal amount of water (45 ml) to make a paste

Grilled Elk

- 3 pounds (1.4 kg) elk, deer, or venison top round, cleaned thoroughly

- Salt

- Cracked black pepper

Directions

Bring red wine to a boil in a 2-quart (1.9 liter) saucepan and reduce by three-fourths. Add beef broth and bring back to a boil. Slowly whisk the gravy mix into the broth until it begins to thicken. (It may not be necessary to use all of the mix.) Reduce heat and simmer 15 to 20 minutes, letting it thicken slowly. Once the mixture reaches the desired consistency, remove from heat. Place rosemary sprig into sauce. Set aside in warm place until needed.

Bring lingonberries and pineapple juice to a boil in a 2-quart (1.9 liter) saucepan. Add ½ cup (100 g) sugar, stir to combine, and reduce heat. Taste to determine if more sugar is necessary. Once compote is to taste, whisk in small amounts of cornstarch mixture until compote thickens a little. (It may not be necessary to use all of the cornstarch mixture.) Simmer gently for 10 minutes to thicken to desired consistency. Remove and cool.

Preheat grill to high. Cut elk into 3- to 4-ounce (85 to 115 g) medallions and sprinkle salt and cracked black pepper on both sides of meat. Grill elk on hot grill to desired doneness. When ready, serve over pool of red wine sauce and top with lingonberry compote. Serve with your favorite vegetable and starch. Scalloped potatoes or roasted red bliss potatoes are a nice accompaniment.

Wine pairing: A full-bodied Cabernet Sauvignon or red Zinfandel is a complementary wine choice.

Fried Alligator

Serves 10

Ingredients

• 5 pounds (2.5 kg) alligator tail, cut into ½-inch (1.25 cm) pieces

• 8 cups (2 liters) milk

• ¾ cup (175 ml) bottled Italian dressing

• 4 tablespoons (60 ml) liquid crab boil (available from Cajun grocers)

• ½ cup (120 ml) hot red pepper sauce

• 2 teaspoons (10 g) prepared mustard

• 2 tablespoons (10 g) Creole-style seasoning mix

• 2 teaspoons (6 g) garlic powder

• 1 cup (235 ml) red wine vinegar

• Flour (or fish fry) for dredging

- Peanut oil for frying

Directions

Mix all ingredients except flour and oil thoroughly in bowl, making certain alligator meat is covered in sauce. Refrigerate at least 24 hours. Drain meat well and roll in flour or fish fry. Heat about 1 tablespoon (15 ml) peanut oil in a frying pan over medium-high heat and fry meat until golden brown and cooked through. Cook in batches, wiping pan out with paper towel between batches.

Alligator Sauce Picante

Serves four to six

Ingredients

- 1½ teaspoons (9 g) salt

- 1 teaspoon (2 g) cayenne pepper

- 1 teaspoon (2 g) black pepper

- ⅓ cup (42 g) flour

- 2 to 3 pounds (1 to 1.5 kg) alligator meat, cleaned and cubed

- Cooking oil as needed

- 1 onion, finely chopped

- 1 (8-ounce/225 g) can diced tomatoes

- Water

- ½ cup (50 g) chopped green onions

- ½ cup (30 g) chopped parsley

Directions

Combine salt, cayenne pepper, black pepper, and flour in a large bowl. Toss alligator meat in flour mixture to coat.

Heat a few tablespoons oil in heavy Dutch oven until smoking and add flour-coated alligator meat. Do not crowd the pan. Cook in batches if needed. The meat will become watery at first; continue cooking over high heat until all water evaporates. Fry until light brown. Transfer meat to another bowl and keep warm until all the alligator meat is cooked.

Add onion to the pan and sauté until translucent. Add tomatoes and cook for 5 minutes. Add water if the mixture becomes too dry. Return the alligator meat to the pan and toss with vegetables. Add green onions and parsley.

Serve over hot cooked rice.

Elk Enchiladas

Serves 8 to 10

Ingredients

- 1-pound (450 g) ground elk

- 1 medium onion, chopped

- Salt and pepper

- 8 to 10 (8-inch/20 cm) flour tortillas

- 1 (15-ounce/425 g) can chili without beans

- 2 (12 ounce/340 g) cans tomato sauce

- 3 cups (340 g) shredded four-cheese

• Mexican blend or Colby/Jack cheese

Directions

Preheat oven to 350°F (180°C). In a large (12-inch/30 cm) frying pan set over high heat, brown ground elk and onions, season with salt and pepper, drain, and set aside.

Wrap flour tortillas in a dish towel and warm in microwave a few seconds. Mix chili and tomato sauce in large glass or ceramic bowl. Microwave for 1 minute.

Pour some chili mixture in bottom of 9 x 13-inch (23 x 33 cm) baking dish. Fill each tortilla with heaping tablespoon of meat mixture and top with equal amount of cheese. Roll up and place seam-side down in baking dish. Repeat until dish is full. Pour remaining chili mixture over enchiladas and top with remaining cheese. Bake for about 30 minutes or until bubbly.

Game Meatballs

Serves to 8

Ingredients

Meatballs

- 3 pounds (1.4 kg) ground game meat (elk, buffalo, and/or deer are recommended)
- 1 (12-ounce/355 ml) can evaporated milk
- 1 cup (80 g) rolled oats (oatmeal)
- 1 cup (50 g) cracker crumbs of your choice
- 2 eggs
- ½ cup (80 g) chopped onions
- ½ tablespoon (4 g) garlic powder
- 2 tablespoons (36 g) salt
- ½ tablespoon (3 g) ground black pepper
- 2 tablespoons (15 g) chili powder

Sauce

- 2 cups (470 ml) ketchup
- 1 cup (220 g) brown sugar
- ½ teaspoon (2.5 ml) liquid smoke
- ½ teaspoon (1.5 g) garlic powder
- ¼ cup (40 g) chopped onions

Directions

Preheat oven to 350°F (180°C). Combine all meatball ingredients. Mix gently to incorporate. Do not overmix. Make into golf ball–sized meatballs. Place in greased baking dish.

Combine sauce ingredients, mix well, and pour over meatballs. Bake in preheated oven for 1 hour.

Game Marinade

Makes enough for 3- to 4-pounds (1.4 to 1.8 kg) meat

Ingredients

- ½ cup (120 ml) olive oil

- ½ cup (120 ml) white wine

- ½ cup (120 ml) soy sauce

- 4½ (67 ml) tablespoons honey

- 6 large garlic cloves, minced

- 3 tablespoons (5 g) chopped fresh rosemary, or 1 tablespoon (3 g) dried

- 1½ tablespoons (10 g) coarsely ground black pepper

- 1½ tablespoons (27 g) sea salt

Directions

Combine all ingredients in a large resealable plastic bag and mix well. Add meat to bag. Push out excess air, seal, and refrigerate for several hours or overnight.

This simple marinade can be used with your favorite game, whether you roast, grill, or sauté.

Smothered Elk Steaks

Serves four

Ingredients

- 4 (8-ounce/227 g) elk strip steaks

- Salt and pepper

- Flour for dredging

- 1 tablespoon (15 ml) vegetable oil

- 12 ounces (336 ml) Chardonnay

- 2 (10.75-ounce/305 g) cans cream of mushroom soup

- 1 envelope beef-flavored dry onion soup

- 1 large onion, sliced very thin, rings separated

- Several fresh mushrooms, sliced

Directions

Using a very sharp knife, cut crisscross patterns about 1 /8-inch (3 mm) deep on both sides of steaks. Season with salt and pepper. Dredge in flour, being sure to shake off excess flour.

Heat vegetable oil in a nonstick frying pan (an electric skillet can be used) and brown the steaks thoroughly on both sides. After the second side has browned, add half the wine and boil for 3 to 4 minutes. Mix soups together with remaining wine. Add this to top of steaks, cover with onion rings and mushrooms, then cover pan and let simmer for 2 to 3 hours, or until steaks are tender.

Mashed potatoes, seasoned green beans, and warm hot rolls make great accompaniments.

Where's It from and What's It Taste Like?

Elk are from North America, Europe, and Asia. The meat is mild and similar to beef but with a bit of a sweet flavor and a faint taste of deer venison. You can easily substitute elk in recipes that call for deer venison.